LODI MEMORIAL LIBRARY, NJ

3 9139 09039665 7

DISCARD

D1709086

WHAT DID THE
TREE
SEE?

W

EDITIONS

Property of
Lodi Memorial Library

For Di and Julian.
S.U.

For my sister, Emma.
C.G.

Published in 2020 by Welbeck Editions
An Imprint of Welbeck Children's Limited,
part of Welbeck Publishing Group.

20 Mortimer Street London W1T 3JW

Text © 2020 Charlotte Guillain
Illustration © 2020 Sam Usher

All rights reserved. No part of this publication
may be reproduced, stored in a retrieval system,
or transmitted in any form or by any means,
electronically, mechanical, photocopying, recording
or otherwise, without the prior permission of the
copyright owners and the publishers.

ISBN 978 1 91351 905 6

Printed with soy inks

Printed in Heshan, China

10 9 8 7 6 5 4 3 2 1

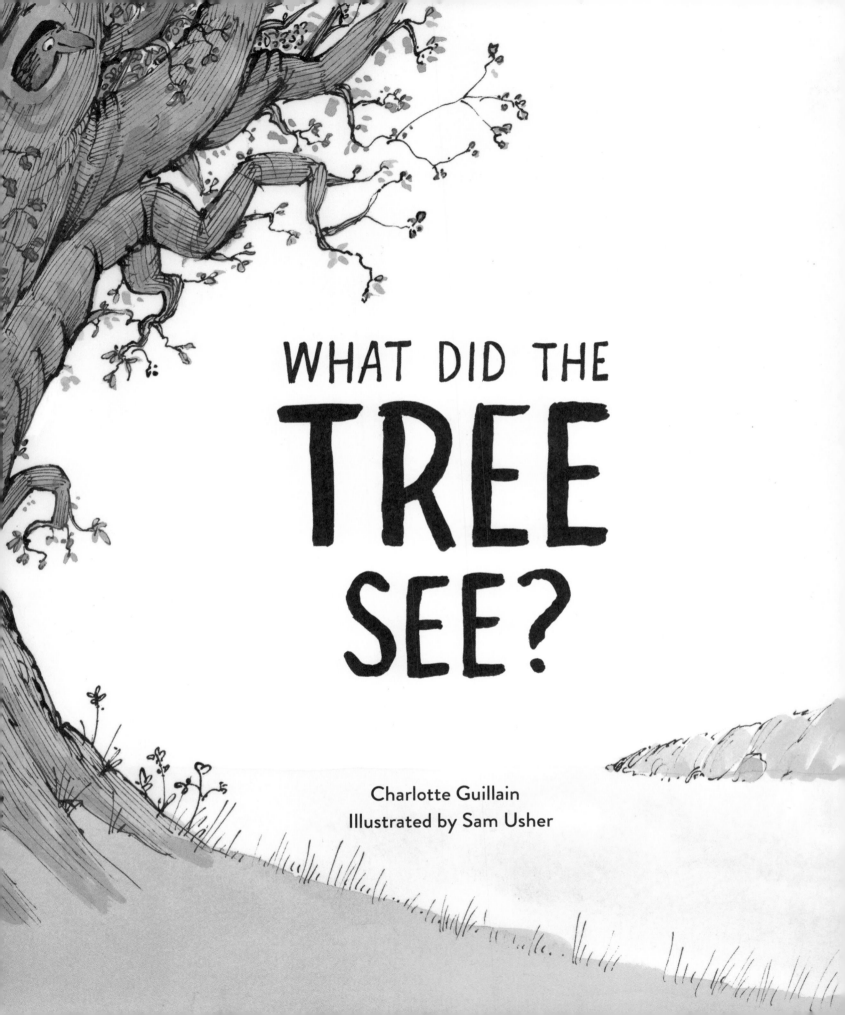

WHAT DID THE TREE SEE?

Charlotte Guillain

Illustrated by Sam Usher

I first was an acorn, so tiny and round,
I fell from a branch and sank into the ground.
Then as I grew up, I turned into a tree...
over hundreds of years! So, what did I see?

When I was a sapling, still growing my bark,
trees shot up around me—we filled a huge park.
My tender young leaves would be nibbled by deer,
but they ran away when the hunters came near.

For years, I grew bigger. My roots reached and spread.
My branches got thicker and stretched overhead.
Some trees were cut down and the forest was cleared.
More people arrived and a village appeared.

Time passed, I got older. My trunk grew and grew,
a ring for each year, where my wood was brand new.
The land all around me was plowed up and sown.
The people worked hard when the crops were all grown.

I watched as the seasons passed by every year.
I felt old leaves fall and new acorns appear.
I heard axes strike as men chopped down more trees,
to build into ships that would sail on the seas.

Property of
Lodi Memorial Library

Then houses were built where the trees were cut down.
I watched as the village changed into a town.
Next, huge, hulking factories rose into view,
and ate up the land as the town grew and grew.

The next thing I knew, there were tracks on the ground,
strange clouds in the air and a whistling sound!
I shook as a steam train came thundering past.
Of all of the oak trees, now I was the last.

My trunk became hollow, but I was still strong,
my branches still rang with the sound of birdsong.
Then diggers arrived and a motorway came
The animals left, but I stayed just the same.

I looked at the sky as planes roared overhead,
the hedgerows were gone and the meadows were dead.
But still children came and they sat in my shade,
they climbed on my branches and happily played.

So now I am ancient and stand on my own.
But look! On my branches new acorns have grown.
And when one falls down and grows into a tree,
Who knows, just imagine it...

...what will it see?

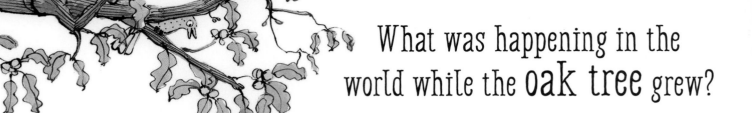

What was happening in the world while the **oak tree** grew?

1000 CE — Viking Leif Erikson sails from Europe to North America.

1066 — William of Normandy in France conquers England and becomes the English king.

1088 — The first university opens in Bologna, Italy, beginning a trend toward higher learning.

1211 — The Mongolian emperor Genghis Khan invades China.

1271–5 — Marco Polo travels from Venice to China.

1347–51 — Millions of people in Europe die from the bubonic plague known as the Black Death.

1438 — The Incas rule a vast civilization in Peru, lasting until 1533.

1455 — In Germany, Johannes Gutenberg uses his newly invented printing press to print the Bible.

1492 — Christopher Columbus sails from Spain to North America.

1497 — Portuguese explorer Vasco da Gama sails around Africa and on to India.

1501 — Slaves begin to be transported from Africa to the Americas; a practice that continues for more than 350 years.

1564 — In England, world-renowned playwright William Shakespeare is born.

1588 — The English defeat the Spanish Armada.

1607 — The first English colony on the American mainland is set up at Jamestown.

1610 — The scientist Galileo sees Jupiter's moons through his telescope.

1666 — The Great Fire of London destroys much of the city.

1703 — A huge storm destroys oak forests all over England. New oaks were planted to provide timber for shipbuilding until well into the 19th century.

1765 — James Watt invents the steam engine.

1776 — The American Revolution ends with the Declaration of Independence.

1789 — The French Revolution begins. George Washington becomes US President.

1793 — Eli Whitney invents the cotton gin, a machine that separates cotton fibers from seeds, speeding up production.

1804 — Napoleon becomes Emperor of France.

1814 — The English inventor George Stephenson invents the first steam locomotive.

1831 — The mechanical reaper is invented, changing the way crops are harvested.

1845–9 Millions die from famine when the potato crop fails in Ireland.

1859 Charles Darwin publishes his book *On the Origin of Species*, introducing the theory of natural selection and evolution.

1861 The American Civil War begins, lasting until 1865.

1865 Slavery is abolished in the United States.

1876 In Germany, Nikolaus Otto invents the internal combustion engine using burning fuel instead of steam to move an engine.

1885 The first skyscraper is built in Chicago. The first car is built in Germany by Karl Benz.

1893 New Zealand is the first country in the world where women can vote.

1903 The American Wright brothers fly in the first airplane.

1908 The American engineer Henry Ford starts to mass-produce cars.

1914 World War I starts and lasts until 1918.

1929 The US stock market crashes and the Great Depression begins.

1939 World War II begins when Hitler invades Poland.

1945 World War II ends. The USA drops atomic bombs on Japan. The United Nations is set up.

1952 Elizabeth II becomes queen of the United Kingdom.

1953 Edmund Hillary and Tenzing Norgay are the first people to stand on the summit of Mount Everest.

1959 The silicon chip is invented, ushering in the modern computer era.

1961 The Russian cosmonaut Yuri Gagarin becomes the first human in space.

1969 American astronaut Neil Armstrong is the first human to walk on the moon.

1989 The Berlin Wall comes down and communist rule ends in central and eastern Europe. Tim Berners-Lee invents the World Wide Web.

1990 Nelson Mandela is freed from jail as apartheid ends in South Africa.

2007 The Tesla Roadster electric car goes into production, one of many new electric cars that emit less pollution and greenhouse gases than gasoline and diesel cars.

2018 Greta Thunberg begins her school strike for climate, sparking protests against climate change across the globe.

2020 The Covid-19 virus pandemic spreads across the world, with many people living under lockdown for weeks at a time.

The life cycle of an oak tree

←Seedling→ ←Formative→ ←Mature→

1. Seedling stage

The oak's fruit is the acorn. It grows in a little cup and turns from green to brown as it ripens. New oak trees grow from acorns. Squirrels and a type of bird called a jay help new oaks to grow by burying acorns to eat later. If they forget where they buried an acorn, it starts to grow! A shoot rises up to find sunlight and a root grows down to find water. In a few months it will be an infant oak, with several leaves. These leaves make food using sunlight, helping the seedling to grow.

2. Formative stage

This stage lasts about 100 years. During this stage, all parts of the tree grow: the branches, the crown where the leaves grow, the trunk, and the roots. First the roots need to expand, so the growing tree can get enough water and hold itself steady in the ground. More leaves produce more food so then the rest of the tree can grow larger. The tree's crown expands to its largest size when it is 80 to 120 years old.

4. Veteran stage

This is when the oak starts to decay, usually because fungus is spreading in the old wood at the heart of the tree's trunk. Some veteran oaks have hollow trunks where this has happened. A veteran oak can still repair itself and remain strong. Even oaks this ancient can produce healthy acorns – they can reproduce for at least 800 years!

← —— Veteran —— →   ← —————— Senescent —————— →

3. Mature stage

The oak tree reaches this stage when its root and crown have finished expanding. Every year, a new ring of wood is added to the trunk and branches, so the tree still grows but the crown does not get bigger. In spring, the tree makes lots of new wood. Later in the year, it grows more slowly, making denser wood. The oak's mature stage can last for hundreds of years.

5. Senescent stage

Now the tree is dying. Its trunk and branches are breaking and rotting and are eaten by bugs living in the tree. The outer shell of the trunk and larger branches can stay strong, so the tree remains standing for a very long time. The tree's crown becomes much smaller now. The tree is finally dead when no new twigs or leaves grow. This can be up to 1,000 years after the acorn first started to grow.

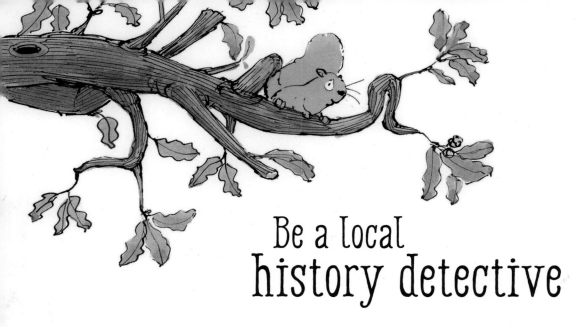

Be a local history detective

Wherever you live, some things around you will have changed over time and others will have stayed the same. Why not be a local history detective and find out more about the places around you?

Go to your local museum or library or look on the internet to find photographs of your local town, city, or village. Do you recognize what you see in the photos? Go for a walk around the place where you live and see what has changed since those pictures were taken.

If you can find any old maps of your local area, compare them with a modern map to see what roads and buildings are new where you live. Has the number of trees in your area changed? Can you find any woods shown on the modern map and go for a walk there?

What are the oldest buildings in your local area? Can you find out what they have been used for over the years? Take a photo or draw a picture of one of these old buildings and record what you can find out about its history.

Talk to older relatives or neighbours about what life was like in your local area when they were younger. What is different now? Find out which shops and jobs there used to be that don't exist anymore. What has replaced them?

Be a friend to the trees

How much attention do you pay to the trees you pass every day? The more we notice trees and the rest of nature around us, the more we will realize how important they are and the more amazing discoveries we will make!

Find an old tree in your local area. You could make a rubbing of its bark—hold a sheet of paper against the trunk and rub a crayon or charcoal against it. You'll be left with the pattern of the bark on the paper. Draw a picture of its leaves. You can look in a book or on the internet to identify the tree if you're not sure what it is. Can you see any birds or animals living among its roots or branches? What bugs can you spot? Go back to the tree at another time of year—what do you notice is different? Take photos to record the changes.

Find out if there is a project to plant more trees where you live. Get involved and watch the new trees grow through the changing seasons. You could look at the National Forest Foundation's website to find out more about how important tree planting is: www.nationalforests.org/get-involved/tree-planting-programs